THE

SEVEN VALLEYS

The quest of the lover for his beloved, of the true seeker for the path to enlightenment, this is the journey through *The Seven Valleys* of Bahá'u'lláh. Written in the mystical tradition of the Ṣúfí poets, it recounts the odyssey of the human soul as it travels from the plain of creation to the sphere of the absolute, its ultimate goal: reunion with God.

With its rich poetic style and metaphorical allusions to the great Ṣúfí writers, this vivid portrayal of the spiritual pilgrimage conveys the timeless verities of faith to guide and inspire the soul.

Books in this series

The Hidden Words of Bahá'u'lláh

The Seven Valleys of Bahá'u'lláh

THE

SEVEN VALLEYS

BY

BAHÁ'U'LLÁH

ONEWORLD
OXFORD

Oneworld Publications Ltd
(Sales and Editorial)
185 Banbury Road
Oxford OX2 7AR, England

Oneworld Publications Ltd
(U.S. Sales Office)
County Route 9, P.O. Box 357
Chatham, NY 12037, U.S.A.

Translated by 'Alí-Kuli Khán, assisted by Marzieh Gail
This edition © Oneworld Publications Ltd 1992
All rights reserved. Copyright under Berne Convention

A CIP record for this book is available from the British Library

ISBN 1-85168-031-4

Book design and cover illustration by Michael W. Sours
Printed and bound in Great Britain by
The Guernsey Press Co. Ltd., Guernsey, Channel Islands.

INTRODUCTION

The *Haft-Vadí*, or *Seven Valleys*, is a beautiful mystical essay revealing the innermost essentials of the seeker's quest to attain access to the Inaccessible – 'God'. It was written by Bahá'u'lláh probably some time in the late 1850's and is contained within a letter to an inquisitive and knowledgeable Shaykh by the name of Muhyí'd-Dín. Bahá'u'lláh (Arabic: lit. *The Glory of God*) was the Prophet-Founder of the Bahá'í Faith, which since its beginnings in 1863 has become a world religion.

However, at the time of this correspondence Bahá'u'lláh had not made His messianic claims known. In fact, the Shaykh may have first known Bahá'u'lláh by the name Darvísh Muhammad-i-Írání. Prior to His proclamation and active public ministry, Bahá'u'lláh had taken this name during a period of withdrawal and seclusion in the desolate mountains of Kurdistán. For two years (April 10, 1854-March 19, 1856) He lived there in a state of material destitution, and in His words, communed with God ('My spirit') 'oblivious of the world and all that is therein'. This period of withdrawal was perhaps in some ways equivalent to Jesus' withdrawal into the wilderness. During this time those who chanced to come into contact with Him were greatly impressed by His sanctity of character and profound mystical knowledge. His reputation spread and soon many individuals sought Him out in the hope of benefiting from His spiritual insight.

The Shaykh, Muḥyí'd-Dín, was one such admirer of Bahá'u'lláh who enjoyed a friendly and respectful contact with Him. The Shaykh was also apparently well acquainted with the writings of certain Muslim mystics. In reading *The Seven Valleys* of Bahá'u'lláh, we are in fact reading a lengthy reply to a letter from Shaykh Muḥyí'd-Dín. He had already written to Bahá'u'lláh sharing with Him his own ideas and interpretations of mystic thought and literature. He had also sought from Bahá'u'lláh answers to questions about certain mystical poems. In particular, it appears that he enquired about what is often referred to as the mystical journey of the seeker from the plain of creation to the sphere of the Absolute (God).

Judging by the structure of, and references in, Bahá'u'lláh's reply it is apparent that He chose to express His answers in the terminology and form familiar to those who were acquainted with Islamic mystical literature. The dominating centrepiece of His letter to the Shaykh uses, as its primary vehicle of expression, the metaphor of seven valleys found in the concluding portion of Farídu'd-Dín 'Attár's most famous and much loved work, *The Conference of the Birds (Manteq at-Tair)*.* Among some Muslim

*Bahá'u'lláh follows 'Attár's structure in so far as He uses the same metaphorical seven valleys. The order of two valleys is reversed but this does not appear to have a bearing on the overall differences that exist between 'Attár's work and Bahá'u'lláh's. The main concluding points suggested by 'Attár's version do not necessarily contradict any of the teachings of Bahá'u'lláh. For example, in 'Attár's account the birds journey towards their goal and in the last stage realize that the object of their quest lies within themselves. In one of Bahá'u'lláh's best known works, *The Hidden Words*, He writes: 'Turn thy sight unto thyself, that thou mayest find Me standing within thee, mighty, powerful and self-subsisting'. However, taken in isolation, this spiritual truth can be interpreted in an exclusively monist way, denying all duality or separation between God and creation, and thus denying any need for the individual to turn to God's Prophets and Messengers as mediators. It is possible to interpret Bahá'u'lláh's *Seven Valleys* as a treatise which gives balance to this point by emphasizing the complete transcendence of God and the need to recognize the Prophets as intermediaries between the world of creation and God. For a brief examination of the significance and origin of the metaphor of the seven valleys, see note 10, p. 64.

mystics, 'Aṭṭár's work was regarded as a poetic exposition of the most important and deepest truths enshrined in the Holy Books, and particularly the Qur'án. 'Aṭṭár's writings, like those of Ḥáfiẓ and Rúmí and other well-known mystics, gained among some an authority and importance second only to the sacred Qur'án itself, even as St Augustine's *City of God*, and the writings of other early Church Fathers, once carried a respect sometimes equal to the inspired writings of Jesus' Apostles.

In some ways Bahá'u'lláh's *Seven Valleys* can be viewed as essentially a restatement, affirmation and clarification of mystical truth and the mystical path. Throughout the world, mystics in all the great religious traditions have shared three principal concerns: purgation, illumination and union. Generally speaking, mystics have all recognized that purgation from the things of this world and sanctification are necessary to attain right spiritual knowledge or illumination. It is through these twin steps of purgation and illumination that the mystic seeker hopes to attain his or her ultimate goal: union with the absolute and eternal Reality. These three perennial elements of mysticism are all affirmed in Bahá'u'lláh's teachings. Nevertheless, along the way of this spiritual journey, many mystics have mistaken one or another aspect or stage of the journey for the final goal itself, or in trying to describe the indescribable, led others to conceive of the Absolute according to their own limited imaginations.

As Bahá'u'lláh affirms and restates the universal truths of the mystic path, He therefore overturns certain pantheistic and anthropomorphic concepts and beliefs which some mystics have fallen into along their journey.* Such ideas are seen as incompatible with God's true reality, which is portrayed as completely exalted beyond all corporeal limitations and is hence inaccessible. Bahá'u'lláh affirms the seeker's need to become sanctified from all material attachments and intellectual limitations that can prevent him or her from attaining to the presence of God, but He indicates that one can only attain the divine presence or union with God, by recognizing God's Manifestation and submitting to His will.

This is perhaps, the most distinguishing characteristic and the central objective of

---

*It was characteristic of Bahá'u'lláh to delineate what He thought were both the sound and unsound realms of mystic thought when asked to comment on the treatises of others (Shoghi Effendi, *God Passes By* 122).

Bahá'u'lláh's discourse concerning the mystical journey. By 'perpetual union with God' is meant that men should merge their will wholly in the will of God. Knowledge of God's will is revealed through God's designated Messengers. As the needs of every age are different, God reveals how His will is to be expressed in a way that is suitable for each age. To know and follow God's will, one must therefore recognize the 'Manifestation', or Messenger of God, for the age one is living in. This is why all the Manifestations have indicated that there is no other 'way' except through them.

The object of the mystic path is therefore to become sanctified from whatever hinders the seeker from recognizing and understanding the teachings and example of God's Manifestation for the age we are living in. The bounty and importance of recognizing God's Manifestations is therefore the distinguishing feature of Bahá'u'lláh's exposition. However, though Ṣúfí thought had derived its greatest inspiration from the revealed Scriptures of Muḥammad, and to a lesser extent other Holy Books, many Ṣúfís neglected to adequately acknowledge the authority and station of the Individuals who imparted these Revelations of God.

At the time Bahá'u'lláh wrote *The Seven Valleys* to Shaykh Muhyí'd-Dín, religious history stood between the advent of two such dynamic and inspiring Individuals. The Persian Prophet, the Báb (Arabic, lit. *Gate*), had begun a ministry in 1844 announcing the imminent appearance of the One foretold in past Scriptures. The Báb had been executed in 1850 and thousands of His followers slaughtered. Soon Bahá'u'lláh was to announce to a small group of devoted followers that He was the One the Báb had heralded, thus ushering in a new stage in humankind's spiritual evolution.

Praise be to God Who hath made being to come
forth from nothingness; graven upon the tablet
of man the secrets of pre-existence[1]; taught him from
the mysteries of divine utterance that which he knew
not; made him a Luminous Book unto those who
believed and surrendered themselves; caused him to
witness the creation of all things (Kullu Shay'[2]) in this
black and ruinous age, and to speak forth from the
apex of eternity with a wondrous voice in the
Excellent Temple[3]: to the end that every man may
testify, in himself, by himself, in the station of the
Manifestation of his Lord, that verily there is no God
save Him, and that every man may thereby win his
way to the summit of realities, until none shall

contemplate anything whatsoever but that he shall see God therein.

And I praise and glorify the first sea which hath branched from the ocean of the Divine Essence, and the first morn which hath glowed from the Horizon of Oneness, and the first sun which hath risen in the Heaven of Eternity, and the first fire which was lit from the Lamp of Pre-existence in the lantern of singleness: He who was Aḥmad[4] in the kingdom of the exalted ones, and Muḥammad amongst the concourse of the near ones, and Maḥmúd in the realm of the sincere ones. ". . . by whichsoever (name) ye will, invoke Him: He hath most excellent names"[5] in the hearts of those who know. And upon His household and companions be abundant and abiding and eternal peace![6]

Further, we have harkened to what the nightingale of knowledge sang on the boughs of the tree of thy being, and learned what the dove of certitude cried on the branches of the bower of thy heart. Methinks I verily inhaled the pure fragrances of the garment of thy love, and attained thy very meeting from perusing thy letter. And since I noted thy mention of thy death in God, and thy life through Him, and thy love for the beloved of God and the Manifestations of His Names and the Dawning-Points of His Attributes - I therefore reveal unto thee sacred and resplendent tokens from the planes of glory, to attract thee into the court of holiness and nearness and beauty, and draw thee to a station wherein thou shalt see nothing in creation save the Face of thy Beloved One, the Honoured, and behold all created things only as in the day wherein none hath a mention.

Of this hath the nightingale of oneness sung in the garden of Ghawthíyyih.[7] He saith: "And there shall appear upon the tablet of thine heart a writing of the subtle mysteries of 'Fear God and God will give you knowledge';[8] and the bird of thy soul shall recall the holy sanctuaries of pre-existence and soar on the wings of longing in the heaven of 'walk the beaten paths of thy Lord', and gather the fruits of communion in the gardens of 'Then feed on every kind of fruit'."[9]

By My life, O friend, wert thou to taste of these fruits, from the green garden of these blossoms which grow in the lands of knowledge, beside the orient lights of the Essence in the mirrors of names and attributes - yearning would seize the reins of patience and reserve from out thy hand, and make thy soul to shake with the flashing light, and draw thee from the earthly homeland to the first, heavenly abode in the Centre of Realities, and lift thee to a plane wherein thou wouldst soar in the air even as thou walkest upon the earth, and move over the water as thou runnest on the land. Wherefore, may it rejoice Me, and thee, and whosoever mounteth into the heaven of knowledge, and whose heart is refreshed by this, that the wind of certitude hath blown over the garden of his being, from the Sheba of the All-Merciful.

Peace be upon him
who followeth the Right Path!

And further: The stages that mark the wayfarer's journey from the abode of dust to the heavenly homeland are said to be seven.[10] Some have called these Seven Valleys, and others, Seven Cities. And they say that until the wayfarer taketh leave of self, and traverseth these stages, he shall never reach to the ocean of nearness and union, nor drink of the peerless wine. The first is

The steed of this Valley is patience; without patience the wayfarer on this journey will reach nowhere and attain no goal. Nor should he ever be downhearted; if he strive for a hundred thousand years and yet fail to behold the beauty of the Friend, he should not falter. For those who seek the Ka'bih[11] of "for Us" rejoice in the tidings: "In Our ways will We guide them."[12] In their search, they have stoutly girded up the loins of service, and seek at every moment to journey from the plane of heedlessness into the realm of being. No bond shall hold them back, and no counsel shall deter them.

It is incumbent on these servants that they cleanse the heart - which is the wellspring of divine treasures - from every marking, and that they turn away from imitation, which is following the traces of their forefathers and sires, and shut the door of friendliness and enmity upon all the people of the earth.[13]

In this journey the seeker reacheth a stage wherein he seeth all created things wandering distracted in search of the Friend. How many a Jacob will he see, hunting after his Joseph; he will behold many a lover, hasting to seek the Beloved, he will witness a world of desiring ones searching after the One Desired. At every moment he findeth a weighty matter, in every hour he becometh aware of a mystery; for he hath taken his heart away from both worlds, and set out for the Ka'bih of the Beloved. At every step, aid from the Invisible Realm will attend him and the heat of his search will grow.

One must judge of search by the standard of the Majnún of Love.[14] It is related that one day they came upon Majnún sifting the dust, and his tears flowing down. They said, "What doest thou?" He said, "I seek for Laylí". They cried, "Alas for thee! Laylí is of pure spirit, and thou seekest her in the dust!" He said, "I seek her everywhere; haply somewhere I shall find her".

Yea, although to the wise it be shameful to seek the Lord of Lords in the dust, yet this betokeneth intense ardour in searching. "Whoso seeketh out a thing with zeal shall find it."[15]

The true seeker hunteth naught but the object of his quest, and the lover hath no desire save union with his beloved. Nor shall the seeker reach his goal unless he sacrifice all things. That is, whatever he hath seen, and heard, and understood, all must he set at naught, that he may enter the realm of the spirit, which is the City of God.[16] Labour is needed, if we are to seek Him; ardour is needed, if we are to drink of the honey of reunion with Him; and if we taste of this cup, we shall cast away the world.

On this journey the traveller abideth in every land and dwelleth in every region. In every face, he seeketh the beauty of the Friend; in every country he looketh for the Beloved. He joineth every company, and seeketh fellowship with every soul, that haply in some mind he may uncover the secret of the Friend, or in some face he may behold the beauty of the Loved One.

And if, by the help of God, he findeth on this journey a trace of the traceless Friend, and inhaleth the fragrance of the long-lost Joseph from the heavenly messenger,[17] he shall straightway step into

THE VALLEY OF LOVE

and be dissolved in the fire of love. In this city the heaven of ecstasy is upraised and the world-illuming sun of yearning shineth, and the fire of love is ablaze; and when the fire of love is ablaze, it burneth to ashes the harvest of reason.

Now is the traveller unaware of himself, and of aught besides himself. He seeth neither ignorance nor knowledge, neither doubt nor certitude; he knoweth not the morn of guidance from the night of error. He fleeth both from unbelief and faith, and deadly poison is a balm to him. Wherefore 'Attár[18] saith:

> For the infidel, error – for the faithful, faith;
> For 'Attár's heart, an atom of Thy pain.

The steed of this Valley is pain; and if there be no pain this journey will never end. In this station the lover hath no thought save the Beloved, and seeketh no refuge save the Friend. At every moment he offereth a hundred lives in the path of the Loved One, at every step he throweth a thousand heads at the feet of the Beloved.

O My Brother! Until thou enter the Egypt of love, thou shalt never come to the Joseph of the Beauty of the Friend; and until, like Jacob, thou forsake thine outward eyes, thou shalt never open the eye of thine inward being; and until thou burn with the fire of love, thou shalt never commune with the Lover of Longing.[19]

A lover feareth nothing and no harm can come nigh him: Thou seest him chill in the fire and dry in the sea.

A lover is he who is chill in hell fire;
A knower is he who is dry in the sea.[20]

Love accepteth no existence and wisheth no life: He seeth life in death, and in shame seeketh glory. To merit the madness of love, man must abound in sanity; to merit the bonds of the Friend, he must be full of spirit. Blessed the neck that is caught in His noose, happy the head that falleth on the dust in the pathway of His love. Wherefore, O friend, give up thy self that thou mayest find the Peerless One, pass by this mortal earth that thou mayest seek a home in the nest of heaven. Be as naught, if thou wouldst kindle the fire of being and be fit for the pathway of love.

Love seizeth not upon a living soul,
The falcon preyeth not on a dead mouse.[20]

Love setteth a world aflame at every turn, and he wasteth every land where he carrieth his banner. Being hath no existence in his kingdom; the wise wield no command within his realm. The leviathan of love swalloweth the master of reason and destroyeth the lord of knowledge. He drinketh the seven seas, but his heart's thirst is still unquenched, and he saith, "Is there yet any more?"[21] He shunneth himself and draweth away from all on earth.

> Love's a stranger to earth and heaven too;
> In him are lunacies seventy-and-two.[22]

He hath bound a myriad victims in his fetters, wounded a myriad wise men with his arrow. Know that every redness in the world is from his anger, and every paleness in men's cheeks is from his poison. He yieldeth no remedy but death, he walketh not save in the valley of the shadow; yet sweeter than honey is his venom on the lover's lips, and fairer his destruction in the seeker's eyes than a hundred thousand lives.

Wherefore must the veils of the satanic self be burned away at the fire of love, that the spirit may

be purified and cleansed and thus may know the
station of the Lord of the Worlds.

> Kindle the fire of love and burn away all
> things,
> Then set thy foot into the land of the lovers.[23]

And if, confirmed by the Creator, the lover escapes
from the claws of the eagle of love, he will enter

THE VALLEY OF KNOWLEDGE

and come out of doubt into certitude, and turn
from the darkness of illusion to the guiding light of
the fear of God. His inner eyes will open and he
will privily converse with his Beloved; he will set
ajar the gate of truth and piety, and shut the doors
of vain imaginings. He in this station is content
with the decree of God, and seeth war as peace, and
findeth in death the secrets of everlasting life. With
inward and outward eyes he witnesseth the mysteries of resurrection in the realms of creation and the
souls of men, and with a pure heart apprehendeth
the divine wisdom in the endless Manifestations of

God. In the ocean he findeth a drop, in a drop he beholdeth the secrets of the sea.

> Split the atom's heart, and lo!
> Within it thou wilt find a sun.[24]

The wayfarer in this Valley seeth in the fashionings of the True One nothing save clear providence, and at every moment saith: "No defect canst thou see in the creation of the God of Mercy: Repeat the gaze: Seest thou a single flaw?"[25] He beholdeth justice in injustice, and in justice, grace. In ignorance he findeth many a knowledge hidden, and in knowledge a myriad wisdoms manifest. He breaketh the cage of the body and the passions, and consorteth with the people of the immortal realm. He mounteth on the ladders of inner truth and hasteneth to the heaven of inner significance. He rideth in the ark of "we shall show them our signs in the regions and in themselves",[26] and journeyeth over the sea of "until it become plain to them that (this Book) is the truth".[26] And if he meeteth with injustice he shall have patience, and if he cometh upon wrath he shall manifest love.

There was once a lover who had sighed for long years in separation from his beloved, and wasted in the fire of remoteness. From the rule of love, his heart was empty of patience, and his body weary of his spirit; he reckoned life without her as a mockery, and time consumed him away. How many a day he found no rest in longing for her; how many a night the pain of her kept him from sleep; his body was worn to a sigh, his heart's wound had turned him to a cry of sorrow. He had given a thousand lives for one taste of the cup of her presence, but it availed him not. The doctors knew no cure for him, and companions avoided his company; yea, physicians have no medicine for one sick of love, unless the favour of the beloved one deliver him.

At last, the tree of his longing yielded the fruit of despair, and the fire of his hope fell to ashes. Then one night he could live no more, and he went out of his house and made for the marketplace. On a sudden, a watchman followed after him. He broke into a run, with the watchman following; then other watchmen came together, and barred every passage to the weary one. And the wretched one cried from his heart, and ran here and there, and moaned to himself: "Surely this watchman is 'Izrá'íl,[27] my angel of death, following so fast upon me; or he is a tyrant of men, seeking to harm me". His feet carried him on, the one bleeding with the arrow of love, and his heart lamented. Then he came to a garden wall, and with untold pain he scaled it, for it proved very high; and forgetting his life, he threw himself down to the garden.

And there he beheld his beloved with a lamp in her hand, searching for a ring she had lost. When the heart-surrendered lover looked on his ravishing love, he drew a great breath and raised up his hands in prayer, crying: "O God! Give Thou glory to the watchman, and riches and long life. For the watchman was Gabriel, guiding this poor one; or he was Isráfíl, bringing life to this wretched one!"

Indeed, his words were true, for he had found many a secret justice in this seeming tyranny of the watchman, and seen how many a mercy lay hid behind the veil. Out of wrath, the guard had led him who was athirst in love's desert to the sea of his loved one, and lit up the dark night of absence with the light of reunion. He had driven one who was afar, into the garden of nearness, had guided an ailing soul to the heart's physician.

Now if the lover could have looked ahead, he would have blessed the watchman at the start, and prayed on his behalf, and he would have seen that tyranny as justice; but since the end was veiled to him, he moaned and made his plaint in the beginning. Yet those who journey in the garden land of knowledge, because they see the end in the beginning, see peace in war and friendliness in anger.

Such is the state of the wayfarers in this Valley; but the people of the Valleys above this see the end and the beginning as one; nay, they see neither beginning nor end, and witness neither "first" nor "last".[28] Nay rather, the denizens of the undying city, who dwell in the green garden land, see not even "neither first nor last"; they fly from all that is first, and repulse all that is last. For these have passed over the worlds of names, and fled beyond the worlds of attributes as swift as lightning. Thus is it said: "Absolute Unity excludeth all attributes".[29] And they have made their dwelling-place in the shadow of the Essence.

Wherefore, relevant to this, Khájih 'Abdu'lláh[30] - may God the Most High sanctify his beloved spirit - hath made a subtle point and spoken an eloquent word as to the meaning of "Guide Thou us on the straight path",[31] which is: "Show us the right way, that is, honour us with the love of Thine Essence, that we may be freed from turning towards ourselves and towards all else save Thee, and may become wholly Thine, and know only Thee, and see only Thee, and think of none save Thee."

Nay, these even mount above this station, wherefore it is said:

> Love is a veil betwixt the lover and the loved
>   one;
> More than this I am not permitted to tell.[32]

At this hour the morn of knowledge hath arisen and the lamps of wayfaring and wandering are quenched.[33]

> Veiled from this was Moses
> Though all strength and light;
> Then thou who hast no wings at all,
> Attempt not flight.[34]

If thou be a man of communion and prayer, soar up on the wings of assistance from Holy Souls, that thou mayest behold the mysteries of the Friend and attain to the lights of the Beloved, "Verily, we are from God and to Him shall we return."[35]

After passing through the Valley of knowledge, which is the last plane of limitation, the wayfarer cometh to

THE VALLEY OF UNITY

and drinketh from the cup of the Absolute, and gazeth on the Manifestations of Oneness. In this station he pierceth the veils of plurality,[36] fleeth from the worlds of the flesh, and ascendeth into the heaven of singleness. With the ear of God he heareth, with the eye of God he beholdeth the mysteries of divine creation. He steppeth into the sanctuary of the Friend, and shareth as an intimate the pavilion of the Loved One. He stretcheth out the hand of truth from the sleeve of the Absolute; he revealeth the secrets of power. He seeth in himself neither name nor fame nor rank, but findeth his own praise in praising God. He beholdeth in his own name the name of God; to him, "all songs are from the King",[37] and every melody from Him. He sitteth on the throne of "Say, all is from God",[38] and taketh his rest on the carpet of "There is no power or might but in God".[39] He looketh on all things with the eye of oneness, and seeth the brilliant rays of the divine sun shining from the dawning-point of Essence alike on all created things, and the lights of singleness reflected over all creation.

It is clear to thine Eminence that all the variations which the wayfarer in the stages of his journey beholdeth in the realms of being, proceed from his own vision.[40] We shall give an example of this, that its meaning may become fully clear: Consider the visible sun; although it shineth with one radiance upon all things, and at the behest of the King of Manifestation bestoweth light on all creation, yet in each place it becometh manifest and sheddeth its bounty according to the potentialities of that place. For instance, in a mirror it reflecteth its own disk and shape, and this is due to the sensitivity of the mirror; in a crystal it maketh fire to appear, and in other things it showeth only the effect of its shining, but not its full disk. And yet, through that effect, by the command of the Creator, it traineth each thing according to the quality of that thing, as thou observest.

In like manner, colours become visible in every object according to the nature of that object. For instance, in a yellow globe, the rays shine yellow; in a white the rays are white; and in a red, the red rays are manifest. Then these variations are from the object, not from the shining light. And if a place be shut away from the light, as by walls or a roof, it will be entirely bereft of the splendour of the light, nor will the sun shine thereon.

Thus it is that certain invalid souls have confined the lands of knowledge within the wall of self and passion, and clouded them with ignorance and blindness, and have been veiled from the light of the mystic sun and the mysteries of the Eternal Beloved; they have strayed afar from the jewelled wisdom of the lucid Faith of the Lord of Messengers, have been shut out of the sanctuary of the All-Beauteous One, and banished from the Ka'bih of splendour. Such is the worth of the people of this age!

And if a nightingale[41] soar upward from the clay of self and dwell in the rose bower of the heart, and in Arabian melodies and sweet Iranian songs recount the mysteries of God - a single word of which quickeneth to fresh, new life the bodies of the dead, and bestoweth the Holy Spirit upon the moldering bones of this existence - thou wilt behold a thousand claws of envy, a myriad beaks of rancour hunting after Him and with all their power intent upon His death.

Yea, to the beetle a sweet fragrance seemeth foul, and to the man sick of a rheum a pleasant perfume is as naught. Wherefore, it hath been said for the guidance of the ignorant:

> Cleanse thou the rheum from out thine head
> And breathe the breath of God instead.[42]

In sum, the differences in objects have now been made plain. Thus when the wayfarer gazeth only upon the place of appearance[43] - that is, when he seeth only the many-coloured globes - he beholdeth yellow and red and white; hence it is that conflict hath prevailed among the creatures, and a darksome dust from limited souls hath hid the world. And some do gaze upon the effulgence of the light; and some have drunk of the wine of oneness and these see nothing but the sun itself.

Thus, for that they move on these three differing planes, the understanding and the words of the wayfarers have differed; and hence the sign of conflict doth continually appear on earth. For some there are who dwell upon the plane of oneness and speak of that world, and some inhabit the realms of limitation, and some the grades of self, while others are completely veiled. Thus do the ignorant people of the day, who have no portion of the radiance of Divine Beauty, make certain claims, and in every age and cycle inflict on the people of the sea of oneness what they themselves deserve.[44] "Should God punish men for their perverse doings, He would not leave on earth a moving thing! But to an appointed term doth He respite them . . ."[45]

O My Brother! A pure heart is as a mirror; cleanse it with the burnish of love and severance from all save God, that the true sun may shine within it and the eternal morning dawn. Then wilt thou clearly see the meaning of "Neither doth My earth nor My heaven contain Me, but the heart of My faithful servant containeth Me".[46] And thou wilt take up thy life in thine hand, and with infinite longing cast it before the new Beloved One.

Whensoever the light of Manifestation of the King of Oneness settleth upon the throne of the heart and soul, His shining becometh visible in

33

every limb and member. At that time the mystery of the famed tradition gleameth out of the darkness: "A servant is drawn unto Me in prayer until I answer him; and when I have answered him, I become the ear wherewith he heareth . . ." For thus the Master of the house[47] hath appeared within His home, and all the pillars of the dwelling are ashine with His light. And the action and effect of the light are from the Light-Giver; so it is that all move through Him and arise by His will. And this is that spring whereof the near ones drink, as it is said: "A fount whereof the near unto God shall drink . . ."[48]

However, let none construe these utterances to be anthropomorphism, nor see in them the descent of the worlds of God into the grades of the creatures; nor should they lead thine Eminence to such assumptions. For God is, in His Essence, holy above ascent and descent, entrance and exit; He hath through all eternity been free of the attributes of human creatures, and ever will remain so. No man hath ever known Him; no soul hath ever found the pathway to His Being. Every mystic knower hath wandered far astray in the valley of the knowledge of Him; every saint hath lost his way in seeking to comprehend His Essence. Sanctified is He above the understanding of the wise; exalted is He above the knowledge of the knowing! The way is barred and to seek it is impiety; His proof is His signs; His being is His evidence.[49]

Wherefore, the lovers of the face of the Beloved have said: "O Thou, the One Whose Essence alone showeth the way to His Essence, and Who is sanctified above any likeness to His creatures".[50] How can utter nothingness gallop its steed in the field of pre-existence, or a fleeting shadow reach to the everlasting sun? The Friend hath said, "But for Thee, we had not known Thee",[51] and the Beloved hath said, "nor attained Thy presence".

Yea, these mentionings that have been made of the grades of knowledge relate to the knowledge of the Manifestations of that Sun of Reality,[52] which casteth Its light upon the Mirrors. And the splendour of that light is in the hearts, yet it is hidden under the veilings of sense and the conditions of this earth, even as a candle within a lantern of iron, and only when the lantern is removed doth the light of the candle shine out.

In like manner, when thou strippest the wrappings of illusion from off thine heart, the lights of oneness will be made manifest.

Then it is clear that even for the rays there is neither entrance nor exit - how much less for that Essence of Being and that longed-for Mystery. O My Brother, journey upon these planes in the spirit of search, not in blind imitation. A true wayfarer will not be kept back by the bludgeon of words nor debarred by the warning of allusions.

> How shall a curtain part the lover and the loved one?
> Not Alexander's wall can separate them![53]

Secrets are many, but strangers are myriad. Volumes will not suffice to hold the mystery of the Beloved One, nor can it be exhausted in these pages, although it be no more than a word, no more than a sign. "Knowledge is a single point, but the ignorant have multiplied it."[54]

On this same basis, ponder likewise the differences among the worlds. Although the divine worlds be never ending, yet some refer to them as four: The world of time (*zamán*), which is the one that hath both a beginning and an end; the world of duration (*dahr*), which hath a beginning, but whose end is not revealed; the world of perpetuity (*sarmad*), whose beginning is not to be seen but which is known to have an end; and the world of eternity (*azal*), neither a beginning nor an end of which is visible. Although there are many differing statements as to these points, to recount them in detail would result in weariness. Thus, some have said that the world of perpetuity hath neither beginning nor end, and have named the world of eternity as the invisible, impregnable Empyrean. Others have called these the worlds of the Heavenly Court (*Láhút*), of the Empyrean Heaven (*Jabarút*), of the Kingdom of the Angels (*Malakút*), and of the mortal world (*Násút*).

The journeys in the pathway of love are reckoned as four: From the creatures to the True One; from the True One to the creatures; from the creatures to the creatures; from the True One to the True One.

There is many an utterance of the mystic seers and doctors of former times which I have not mentioned here, since I mislike the copious citation from sayings of the past; for quotation from the words of others proveth acquired learning, not the divine bestowal. Even so much as We have quoted here is out of deference to the wont of men and after the manner of the friends. Further, such matters are beyond the scope of this epistle. Our unwillingness to recount their sayings is not from pride, rather is it a manifestation of wisdom and a demonstration of grace.

If <u>Kh</u>iḍr did wreck the vessel on the sea,
Yet in this wrong there are a thousand rights.[55]

Otherwise, this Servant regardeth Himself as utterly lost and as nothing, even beside one of the beloved of God, how much less in the presence of His holy ones. Exalted be My Lord, the Supreme! Moreover, our aim is to recount the stages of the wayfarer's journey, not to set forth the conflicting utterances of the mystics.

Although a brief example hath been given concerning the beginning and ending of the relative world, the world of attributes, yet a second illustration is now added, that the full meaning may be manifest. For instance, let thine Eminence consider his own self; thou art first in relation to thy son, last in relation to thy father. In thine outward appearance, thou tellest of the appearance of power in the realms of divine creation; in thine inward being thou revealest the hidden mysteries which are the divine trust deposited within thee. And thus firstness and lastness, outwardness and inwardness are, in the sense referred to, true of thyself, that in these four states conferred upon thee thou shouldst comprehend the four divine states, and that the nightingale of thine heart on all the branches of the rose-tree of existence, whether visible or concealed, should cry out: "He is the first and the last, the Seen and the Hidden . . ."[56]

These statements are made in the sphere of that which is relative, because of the limitations of men. Otherwise, those personages who in a single step have passed over the world of the relative and the limited, and dwelt on the fair plane of the Absolute, and pitched their tent in the worlds of authority and command - have burned away these relativities with a single spark, and blotted out these words with a drop of dew. And they swim in the sea of the spirit, and soar in the holy air of light. Then what life have words, on such a plane, that "first" and "last" or other than these be seen or mentioned! In this realm, the first is the last itself, and the last is but the first.

In thy soul of love build thou a fire
And burn all thoughts and words entire.[57]

O my friend, look upon thyself: Hadst thou not become a father nor begotten a son, neither wouldst thou have heard these sayings. Now forget them all, that thou mayest learn from the Master of Love in the schoolhouse of oneness, and return unto God, and forsake the inner land of unreality[58] for thy true station, and dwell within the shadow of the tree of knowledge.

O thou dear one! Impoverish thyself, that thou mayest enter the high court of riches; and humble thy body, that thou mayest drink from the river of glory, and attain to the full meaning of the poems whereof thou hadst asked.

Thus it hath been made clear that these stages depend on the vision of the wayfarer. In every city he will behold a world, in every valley reach a spring, in every meadow hear a song. But the falcon of the mystic heaven hath many a wondrous carol of the spirit in His breast, and the Persian bird keepeth in His soul many a sweet Arab melody; yet these are hidden, and hidden shall remain.

> If I speak forth, many a mind will shatter,
> And if I write, many a pen will break.[59]

Peace be upon him who
concludeth this exalted journey and followeth the
True One by the lights of guidance.

And the wayfarer, after traversing the high planes of
this supernal journey, entereth

THE VALLEY OF CONTENTMENT

In this Valley he feeleth the winds of divine contentment blowing from the plane of the spirit. He burneth away the veils of want, and with inward and outward eye, perceiveth within and without all things the day of: "God will compensate each one out of His abundance".[60] From sorrow he turneth to bliss, from anguish to joy. His grief and mourning yield to delight and rapture.

Although to outward view, the wayfarers in this Valley may dwell upon the dust, yet inwardly they

41

are throned in the heights of mystic meaning; they eat of the endless bounties of inner significances, and drink of the delicate wines of the spirit.

The tongue faileth in describing these three Valleys, and speech falleth short. The pen steppeth not into this region, the ink leaveth only a blot. In these planes, the nightingale of the heart hath other songs and secrets, which make the heart to stir and the soul to clamour, but this mystery of inner meaning may be whispered only from heart to heart, confided only from breast to breast.

> Only heart to heart can speak the bliss of
>   mystic knowers;
> No messenger can tell it and no missive
>   bear it.[61]
> I am silent from weakness on many a
>   matter,
> For my words could not reckon them
>   and my speech would fall short.[62]

O friend, till thou enter the garden of such mysteries, thou shalt never set lip to the undying wine of this Valley. And shouldst thou taste of it, thou wilt shield thine eyes from all things else, and drink of the wine of contentment; and thou wilt loose thyself from all things else, and bind thyself to Him, and throw thy life down in His path, and cast thy soul away. However, there is no other in this region that thou need forget: "There was God and there was naught beside Him".[63] For on this plane the traveller witnesseth the beauty of the Friend in everything. Even in fire, he seeth the face of the Beloved. He beholdeth in illusion the secret of reality, and readeth from the attributes the riddle of the Essence. For he hath burnt away the veils with his sighing, and unwrapped the shroudings with a single glance; with piercing sight he gazeth on the new creation; with lucid heart he graspeth subtle verities. This is sufficiently attested by: "And we have made thy sight sharp in this day".[64]

After journeying through the planes of pure contentment, the traveller cometh to

THE VALLEY OF WONDERMENT

and is tossed in the oceans of grandeur, and at every moment his wonder groweth. Now he seeth the shape of wealth as poverty itself, and the essence of freedom as sheer impotence. Now is he struck dumb with the beauty of the All-Glorious; again is he wearied out with his own life. How many a mystic tree hath this whirlwind of wonderment snatched by the roots, how many a soul hath it exhausted. For in this Valley the traveller is flung into confusion, albeit, in the eye of him who hath attained, such marvels are esteemed and well beloved. At every moment he beholdeth a wondrous world, a new creation, and goeth from astonishment to astonishment, and is lost in awe at the works of the Lord of Oneness.

Indeed, O Brother, if we ponder each created thing, we shall witness a myriad perfect wisdoms and learn a myriad new and wondrous truths. One of the created phenomena is the dream. Behold how many secrets are deposited therein, how many wisdoms treasured up, how many worlds concealed. Observe, how thou art asleep in a dwelling, and its doors are barred; on a sudden thou findest thyself in a far-off city, which thou enterest without moving thy feet or wearying thy body; without using thine eyes, thou seest; without taxing thine ears, thou hearest; without a tongue, thou speakest. And perchance when ten years are gone, thou wilt witness in the outer world the very things thou hast dreamed tonight.

Now there are many wisdoms to ponder in the dream, which none but the people of this Valley can comprehend in their true elements. First, what is this world, where without eye and ear and hand and tongue a man puts all of these to use? Second, how is it that in the outer world thou seest today the effect of a dream, when thou didst vision it in the world of sleep some ten years past? Consider the difference between these two worlds and the mysteries which they conceal, that thou mayest attain to divine confirmations and heavenly discoveries and enter the regions of holiness.

God, the Exalted, hath placed these signs in men, to the end that philosophers may not deny the mysteries of the life beyond nor belittle that which hath been promised them. For some hold to reason and deny whatever the reason comprehendeth not, and yet weak minds can never grasp the matters which we have related, but only the Supreme, Divine Intelligence can comprehend them:

How can feeble reason encompass the
    Qur'án,
Or the spider snare a phoenix in his web?[65]

45

All these states are to be witnessed in the Valley of Wonderment, and the traveller at every moment seeketh for more, and is not wearied. Thus the Lord of the First and the Last,[66] in setting forth the grades of contemplation and expressing wonderment, hath said: "O Lord, increase my astonishment at Thee!"

Likewise, reflect upon the perfection of man's creation, and that all these planes and states are folded up and hidden away within him.

> Dost thou reckon thyself only a puny form
> When within thee the universe is folded?[67]

Then we must labour to destroy the animal condition, till the meaning of humanity shall come to light.

Thus, too, Luqmán[68], who had drunk from the wellspring of wisdom and tasted of the waters of mercy, in proving to his son Nathan the planes of resurrection and death, advanced the dream as an evidence and an example. We relate it here, that through this evanescent Servant a memory may endure of that youth of the school of Divine Unity, that elder of the art of instruction and the Absolute. He said: "O Son, if thou art able not to sleep, then thou art able not to die. And if thou art able not to waken after sleep, then thou shalt be able not to rise after death."[69]

O friend, the heart is the dwelling of eternal mysteries, make it not the home of fleeting fancies; waste not the treasure of thy precious life in employment with this swiftly passing world. Thou comest from the world of holiness - bind not thine heart to the earth; thou art a dweller in the court of nearness - choose not the homeland of the dust.

In sum, there is no end to the description of these stages, but because of the wrongs inflicted by the peoples of the earth, this Servant is in no mood to continue:

> The tale is still unfinished and I have no
> heart for it -
> Then pray forgive me.[70]

The pen groaneth and the ink sheddeth tears, and the river[71] of the heart moveth in waves of blood. "Nothing can befall us but what God hath destined for us."[72]

Peace be upon him
who followeth the Right Path!

After scaling the high summits of wonderment the wayfarer cometh to

THE VALLEY OF TRUE POVERTY
AND
ABSOLUTE NOTHINGNESS

This station is the dying from self and the living in God, the being poor in self and rich in the Desired One. Poverty as here referred to signifieth being poor in the things of the created world, rich in the things of God's world. For when the true lover and devoted friend reacheth to the presence of the Beloved, the sparkling beauty of the Loved One and the fire of the lover's heart will kindle a blaze and burn away all veils and wrappings. Yea, all he hath, from heart to skin, will be set aflame, so that nothing will remain save the Friend.

> When the qualities of the Ancient of Days[73]
>   stood revealed,
> Then the qualities of earthly things did
>   Moses burn away.[74]

48

He who hath attained this station is sanctified from all that pertaineth to the world. Wherefore, if those who have come to the sea of His presence are found to possess none of the limited things of this perishable world, whether it be outer wealth or personal opinions, it mattereth not. For whatever the creatures have is limited by their own limits, and whatever the True One hath is sanctified therefrom; this utterance must be deeply pondered that its purport may be clear. "Verily the righteous shall drink of a winecup tempered at the camphor fountain."[75] If the interpretation of "camphor" become known, the true intention will be evident. This state is that poverty of which it is said, "Poverty is My glory"[76]. And of inward and outward poverty there is many a stage and many a meaning which I have not thought pertinent to mention here; hence I have reserved these for another time, dependent on what God may desire and fate may seal.

This is the plane whereon the vestiges of all things (Kullu Shay') are destroyed in the traveller, and on the horizon of eternity the Divine Face riseth out of the darkness, and the meaning of "All on the earth shall pass away, but the face of thy Lord . . ."[77] is made manifest.

O My friend, listen with heart and soul to the songs of the spirit, and treasure them as thine own eyes. For the heavenly wisdoms, like the clouds of spring, will not rain down on the earth of men's hearts forever; and though the grace of the All-Bounteous One is never stilled and never ceasing, yet to each time and era a portion is allotted and a bounty set apart, this in a given measure. "And no one thing is there, but with Us are its storehouses; and We send it not down but in settled measure."[78] The cloud of the Loved One's mercy raineth only on the garden of the spirit, and bestoweth this bounty only in the season of spring. The other seasons have no share in this greatest grace, and barren lands no portion of this favour.

O Brother! Not every sea hath pearls; not every branch will flower, nor will the nightingale sing thereon. Then, ere the nightingale of the mystic paradise repair to the garden of God, and the rays of the heavenly morning return to the Sun of Truth - make thou an effort, that haply in this dust-heap of the mortal world thou mayest catch a fragrance from the everlasting garden, and live forever in the shadow of the peoples of this city.[79] And when thou hast attained this highest station and come to this mightiest plane, then shalt thou gaze on the Beloved, and forget all else. ✗

> The Beloved shineth on gate and wall
> Without a veil, O men of vision.[80]

Now hast thou abandoned the drop of life and come to the sea of the Life-Bestower. This is the goal thou didst ask for; if it be God's will, thou wilt gain it.

In this city, even the veils of light are split asunder and vanish away. "His beauty hath no veiling save light, His face no covering save revelation."[81] How strange that while the Beloved is visible as the sun, yet the heedless still hunt after tinsel and base metal. Yea, the intensity of His revelation hath covered Him, and the fullness of His shining forth hath hidden Him.

> Even as the sun, bright hath He shined,
> But alas, He hath come to the town of the
>   blind![82]

In this Valley, the wayfarer leaveth behind him the stages of the "oneness of Being and Manifestation"[83] and reacheth a oneness that is sanctified above these two stations. Ecstasy alone can encompass this theme, not utterance nor argument; and whosoever hath dwelt at this stage of the journey, or caught a breath from this garden land, knoweth whereof We speak.

In all these journeys the traveller must stray not the breadth of a hair from the "Law", for this is indeed the secret of the "Path" and the fruit of the Tree of "Truth"; and in all these stages he must cling to the robe of obedience to the commandments, and hold fast to the cord of shunning all forbidden things, that he may be nourished from the cup of the Law and informed of the mysteries of Truth.[84]

If any of the utterances of this Servant may not be comprehended, or may lead to perturbation, the same must be inquired of again, that no doubt may linger, and the meaning be clear as the Face of the Beloved One shining from the "Glorious Station".[85] These journeys have no visible ending in the world of time, but the severed wayfarer - if invisible confirmation descend upon him and the Guardian of the Cause assist him - may cross these seven stages in seven steps, nay rather in seven breaths, nay rather in a single breath, if God will and desire it. And this is of "His grace on such of His servants as He pleaseth".[86]

They who soar in the heaven of singleness and reach to the sea of the Absolute, reckon this city - which is the station of life in God - as the furthermost state of mystic knowers, and the farthest homeland of the lovers. But to this evanescent One of the mystic ocean, this station is the first gate of the heart's citadel, that is, man's first entrance to the city of the heart; and the heart is endowed with four stages, which would be recounted should a kindred soul be found.

When the pen set to picturing this station,
It broke in pieces and the page was torn.[87]

Salám![88]

O My friend! Many a hound pursueth this gazelle of the desert of oneness; many a talon claweth at this thrush of the eternal garden. Pitiless ravens do lie in wait for this bird of the heavens of God, and the huntsman of envy stalketh this deer of the meadow of love.

O <u>Shaykh</u>! Make of thine effort a glass, perchance it may shelter this flame from the contrary
winds; albeit this light doth long to be kindled in
the lamp of the Lord, and to shine in the globe of
the spirit. For the head raised up in the love of God
will certainly fall by the sword, and the life that is
kindled with longing will surely be sacrificed, and
the heart which remembereth the Loved One will
surely brim with blood. How well is it said:

> Live free of love, for its very peace is
>   anguish;
> Its beginning is pain, its end is death.[89]

Peace be upon him
who followeth the Right Path!

The thoughts thou hast expressed as to the interpretation of the common species of bird that is called in
Persian Gunji<u>sh</u>k (sparrow) were considered.[90]
Thou appearest to be well-grounded in mystic
truth. However, on every plane, to every letter a
meaning is allotted which relateth to that plane.
Indeed, the wayfarer findeth a secret in every name,
a mystery in every letter. In one sense, these letters
refer to holiness.

Káf or *Gáf* (*K* or *G*) referreth to *Kuffi* ("*free*"), that is, "Free thyself from that which thy passion desireth; then advance unto thy Lord".

Nún referreth to *Nazzih* ("*purify*"), that is, "Purify thyself from all else save Him, that thou mayest surrender thy life in His love".

Jím is *Jánib* ("*draw back*"), that is, "Draw back from the threshold of the True One if thou still possessest earthly attributes".

Shín is *Ushkur* ("*thank*") – "Thank thy Lord on His earth that He may bless thee in His heaven; albeit in the world of oneness, this heaven is the same as His earth".

Káf referreth to *Kuffi*, that is: "Take off from thyself the wrappings of limitations, that thou mayest come to know what thou hast not known of the states of Sanctity".[91]

Wert thou to harken to the melodies of this mortal Bird[92], then wouldst thou seek out the undying chalice and pass by every perishable cup.

Peace be upon those
who walk in the Right Path!

NOTES

The study of Bahá'u'lláh's major works suggests that throughout His ministry certain central theological teachings remained thoroughly consistent. For example, He continually stressed that because of the complete transcendence of God, God is only accessible through divine intermediaries such as Moses, Christ, Muhammad and Himself. Many of the teachings unfolded in *The Seven Valleys* are likewise evident in other works such as the *Kitáb-i-Íqán*, one of His earliest works, and the *Lawh-i-Ibn-i-Dhi'b*, (*Epistle to the Son of the Wolf*) His last major work. However, what distinguishes *The Seven Valleys* from works such as the *Kitáb-i-Íqán* is its strong emphasis on popular and well known mystical symbolism and motifs. It appears that the literary dimension of *The Seven Valleys* reflects the mode or vehicle of expression common to eastern mysticism, while the content or objectives reflect the theological teachings common to other writings of Bahá'u'lláh.

With these points in mind, it is apparent that there are two keys that can help us unlock some of the many jewels of meaning contained within the *Seven Valleys*: an acquaintance with Bahá'u'lláh's teachings as explained in His other writings, and familiarity with the stories, symbols and other cultural expressions that He employed to express His teachings. The following notes - which are not part of the original text of Bahá'u'lláh's *Seven Valleys* and which only reflect the opinions and research of the commentator - have been included to aid the reader in the pursuit of these two goals.

I would like to express my thanks to Stephen Lambden, Khazeh Fananapazir, and Vaḥíd Ra'fatí for their assistance on this project. In forming these notes Stephen Lambden was consulted concerning the Arabic of the opening paragraph, Khazeh Fananapazir made helpful suggestions which were included in footnotes 2 and 21, and Vaḥíd Ra'fatí provided information for footnote 7. Most of the references providing numbers for Qur'ánic verses, attributing passages to Imám 'Alí and the poets Rúmí, Aṭṭár and Ḥáfiẓ, have been retained from the 1952 edition.

Michael W. Sours

1. Bahá'u'lláh's son, 'Abdu'l-Bahá, explained that 'the spirit of man *has* a beginning, but it has no end; it continues eternally', whereas the 'reality of prophethood, which is the Word of God and the perfect state of manifestation, did not have any beginning and will not have any end' (*Some Answered Questions* 151-2, emphasis added). Shoghi Effendi explained that 'the passage in "Seven Valleys" referring to pre-existence . . . in no way presupposes the existence of the individual soul before conception'. Referring directly to the original Arabic, he said, 'what is meant is that man's soul is the repository of the ancient, divine mysteries of God' (*from a letter written on behalf of Shoghi Effendi, January 5, 1948*: Helen Hornby, *Lights of Guidance* 375).

2. "Kullu <u>Sh</u>ay' " (lit. all things) refers to the creative activity of God and His power to make all things new. In particular, it has a prophetic significance, referring to the Manifestation of God who renews and revolutionizes human society in each new age. Cf. Qur'án 25:2, 36:12, 41:21; Isaiah 65:17, Revelation 21:5.

3. The Manifestation of God. In many passages Bahá'u'lláh likens, or parallels in significance, the Manifestations such as Moses, Christ, Muḥammad, and Himself to the Temple of God. See, for example, *Kitáb-i-Íqán* 103-4, 153. In some context the Temple signifies the human body. For example,

Bahá'u'lláh writes that God 'hath caused those luminous Gems of Holiness to appear out of the realm of the spirit, in the noble form of the human temple' (*Kitáb-i-Íqán* 99). This equation can also be found in the words of Jesus (John 2:19-21). This passage, therefore, appears to be saying that God has caused Him (God's Mediator) to speak forth from the heights of eternity with a wondrous voice in the noble form of the human temple.

4. The names *Ahmad* (The Most-Praised), and *Mahmúd* (The Glorified), are titles that are used to refer to the Prophet Muhammad, and which, like the name *Muhammad* (The Praised One), are derived from the Arabic verb 'to praise'.

5. Qur'án 17:110.

6. This paragraph expresses a firm recognition of Muhammad while at the same time emphasizing the divine unity of all God's Manifestations. There appears to be an underlying subtlety in the terms: by emphasizing that Muhammad is a manifestation of the 'first' (God), Muhammad is not the last Prophet, as is believed by most Muslims, but rather the manifestation of the Godhead which is both the first and the last. Thus, all Manifestations of God, such as Moses, Christ, Muhammad and now Bahá'u'lláh, are all Manifestations of the 'first' and the 'last'. See *Kitáb-i-Íqán* 161ff. Many Muslims objected to the claims of the Báb and Bahá'u'lláh on the grounds that

Muḥammad was the 'Seal of the Prophets', which they interpreted to mean that no Prophet will appear after Muḥammad.

7. It was previously thought that 'garden of Ghawthíyyíh' referred to a sermon of Imám 'Alí (see 1952 edn.). However, the 'garden of Ghawthíyyíh' probably refers to the words of 'Abdu'l Qádir Jílání, a renowned twelfth-century Islamic theologian, preacher and Súfi (see *Encyclopedia of Islam*, vol. 1, 69). He was widely known as '*Ghawth*', literally 'help', a title of the highest spiritual authority among the hierarchy of Muslim saints (see Annemarie Schimmel, *Mystical Dimensions of Islam* 200). Thus, in this paragraph, Bahá'u'lláh quotes the words of Jílání, who in turn refers to three passages from the Qur'án.

8. Qur'án 2:282. 'But Fear God and God will give you knowledge, for God hath knowledge of all things.' That is, God knows all our doings, therefore we should fear God's judgement. By this fear, we will be obedient to His commandments and gain knowledge of what is good through our own experience. Jalál'u-Dín Rúmí writes, 'God has called Himself 'Alím (Knowing), in order that thou mayest fear to meditate a wicked deed' (*Mathnaví*, Book IV:217).

9. Qur'án 16:71. This particular Qur'ánic passage offers a metaphor that is instructive for the spiritual search. 'And thy Lord hath taught the bee, saying:

". . . Feed, moreover, on every kind of fruit, and walk the beaten paths of thy Lord." From its belly cometh forth a fluid of varying hues [honey], which yieldeth medicine to man. Verily in this is a sign for those who consider'. In the context of the Seven Valleys, one likely meaning is that the seeker should - free from prejudice - 'gather the fruits of communion [with God]' from whatever source they may be found, even as a bee extracts honey from many types of flowers. The bee is an unusual creature in its ability to seek out and find its goal.

10. The seven stages is a traditional Eastern mystical concept used to delineate aspects of the spiritual path to God, in this case expressed as seven stages from 'the abode of dust' (i.e., worldliness, the self, etc.) to 'the heavenly homeland' (i.e., sanctification, divinity, etc.) The use of the metaphor of seven valleys in Islamic mysticism to symbolize the stages of the soul may have been influenced in part by the seven symbolic spheres or heavens mentioned in the Qur'án, which are said to separate the world of creation from the Absolute. This metaphor, which may be derived from the fact that seven planets are visible to the unaided eye, pre-dates the Qur'án, but its inclusion in the sacred text must have enhanced its influence. Thus, in this context, Bahá'u'lláh may be drawing upon an established symbolism based on the ancient astronomical view of the earth at the centre of creation, surrounded by seven spheres representing different levels of heaven. According to this

symbolism, the earth is the lowest plain and the seventh sphere signifies the farthest reaches of 'heaven', the habitation of God. This symbolism lends itself well to the idea of a spiritual progression from the human sphere to the farthest realm of God.

The importance of the number seven goes back to ancient times and is common to many civilisations. In search of a rational explanation, modern scholars generally assume that it was originally derived from the observation of the four phases of the moon in seven-day periods. It is also argued that the significance of the number seven was developed further at a much later date by the awareness of seven planets visible to the unaided eye.

More than a way of structuring mystical thought, the special significance of the number seven is fully incorporated into the religious ordering of society and the language of prophecy. The number seven, as seen in astronomical phenomena, for example, correlates to the ancient Hebrew Sabbath, from which the number seven is given a special sanctity. In biblical Scripture, the last or seventh day of the week is the day of rest (Gen. 2:2-3) and signifies in prophecy the coming Day of God (cf. 2 Pet. 3:8; Rev. 20:2) wherein peace will be established on earth (Heb. 4:8-11) and people will attain the presence of God Himself (Rev. 21:3; Qur'án 18:111; *Kitáb-i-Íqán* 139ff). While *The Seven Valleys* of Bahá'u'lláh is an original work with it own specific message, it is conveyed in the form of a commentary on existing mystical poetry - as was requested by Sha<u>kh</u>

Muḥyí'd-Dín – and it is probably because of the importance and sacredness of the number seven in culture, Scripture and mysticism that Bahá'u'lláh, like others, chooses to retain this form for His own explanation.

11. The Ka'bih (or Kaaba, lit. a Cube) is the place that is the point of adoration of the whole world. In Judaism this was Jerusalem (on account of the Temple, wherein the Presence of God is said to have dwelled among the people, Exodus 40:34ff), and in Islam it is the holy shine in Mecca, which is the point (or Qiblih) to which prayers are offered and a place of pilgrimage for the Muslim world. Even as the Ka'bih is the goal of all pilgrims, the Manifestation is the Ka'bih or goal of all seekers. Bahá'u'lláh likens the station of divinity (*Epistle to the Son of the Wolf* 113) and Himself (ibid. 17, 140) to the Ka'bih. In some cases where He uses the term Qiblih in reference to Himself it has been translated in the Bahá'í writings as 'the Object of the adoration of the world' (e.g., *Tablets of Bahá'u'lláh* 9).

12. A reference to Qur'án 29:69: 'And whoso maketh efforts for Us, in Our ways will We guide them.' Cf. Matt. 7:7-8.

13. In this paragraph Bahá'u'lláh sets forth the essential prerequisites of the true seeker. Cf. *Kitáb-i-Íqán* 3-4, 192ff.

14. The story of Majnún (lit. *insane*) and Laylí is an archetypal love story frequently retold in Persian literature, the most famous version being that of Niẓámí (see *Nazami: The Story of Layla and Majnum*, trans. by Dr. R. Gelpke). Mention can also be found in the *Ma<u>th</u>naví* of Jalálu'd-Dín Rúmí, and this particular episode is described in 'The Valley of the Quest' in 'Aṭṭár's *Conference of the Birds* (see lines 90-1 and 'Aṭṭár's 'The Valley of Love'). Bahá'u'lláh's following comments on the story once again show how much the message of *The Seven Valleys* is expressed in the popular terminology of Ṣúfi thought.

15. Arabian Proverb.

16. 'The City of God' is a popular symbol for all the great religious traditions of the West. It gained prominence in prophetic Scripture after the decline of Jerusalem and reflected hope for the restoration of its glory. It becomes especially central to the millennial hopes expressed in the Book of Revelation (Rev. 21), which speaks of a New Jerusalem, 'the great city, the holy Jerusalem, descending out of heaven from God'. See also Hebrews 12:22-4. Bahá'u'lláh frequently equates the imagery of this heavenly city with the Word of God and the divine Law revealed in each age (*Kitáb-i-Íqán* 199-200). The recognition of the Word and submission to its teachings signifies entrance into the City of God and the attainment of the seeker's goal. See *Kitáb-i-Íqán* 196ff.

17. This is an allusion to the story of Joseph as told in the Old Testament (Gen. ch. 37ff) and the Qur'án (the Surah of Joseph) and which is frequently alluded to in Bahá'í teachings. Shoghi Effendi pointed out in his book *God Passes By* that the story of how Joseph is betrayed by his jealous brothers prefigures the betrayal by Mírzá Yahyá (Bahá'u'lláh's half-brother) of Bahá'u'lláh (p. 23). The first commentary (entitled *Qayyúmu'l-Asmá*') that the Báb wrote at the beginning of His ministry was on the Surah of Joseph and contains passages anticipating the appearance of Bahá'u'lláh. (See *Kitáb-i-Íqán* 231. See also footnote 19 below.)

18. Farídu'd-Dín 'Attár (c. 1150-1230 AD) the Persian Súfi poet and author of *The Conference of the Birds*.

19. This is a reference to the Qur'ánic version of the story of Jacob and his son Joseph (Qur'án 12:93). The scent of Joseph's garment is said to have restored Jacob's sight. Here, the fragrance of Joseph's garment is used as a metaphor signifying Joseph's holiness. Even as a garment is used to adorn the physical body, divine virtues adorn the character of the faithful believer (see *Gleanings* 81). As mentioned in note 16, Bahá'u'lláh likens Himself to the true Joseph who was betrayed by His brothers. The metaphor of the fragrance of His garment is used frequently in the Scriptures of Bahá'u'lláh. Bahá'u'lláh writes, 'Methinks at this moment, I catch the fragrance of

His garment blowing from the Egypt of Bahá' (*The Four Valleys* 56). (See also, e.g., *Tablets of Bahá'u'lláh* 220 and *Gleanings* 30. Cf. Gen. 27:27.) The story of Joseph is frequently mentioned in Ṣúfí mystical writings such as 'Aṭṭár's *Conference of the Birds*.

20. Persian mystic poem.

21. Cf. Qur'án 50:29. This verse refers to Hell saying, 'Is there yet any more'. However, in this context it is being used in an idiomatic way to refer to the condition of the seeker who constantly seeks for more (i.e., knowledge/nearness to God, etc.). In Persian and Arabic literature the verse is used to express the state of seeking.

22. From the *Mathnaví* of Jalálu'd-Dín Rúmí (1207–73 AD).

23. From an ode by Bahá'u'lláh.

24. Persian mystic poem.

25. Qur'án 67:3.

26. Qur'án 41:53.

27. In Islamic tradition, 'Izrá'íl is often thought of as the angel of death. There are many inconsistencies concerning the number and role of angels in Jewish, Christian and Islamic legends. However, in

Islamic thought 'Izrá'íl is grouped as one of the four archangels: Mikhá'íl (Michael), Jibríl (Gabriel), 'Izrá'íl and Isráfíl. This may reflect the description in the Book of Enoch that out of the seven archangels (Enoch chaps. 40ff) there are four angels 'of the Throne' (Michael, Gabriel, Raphael and Fanuel). Sometimes 'Izrá'íl is given the office of trumpet-blower at the last Judgement, other times this same office is given to Isráfíl. In *The Seven Valleys* it appears that 'Izrá'íl signifies the angel of death and, in the following paragraph, Isráfíl signifies an angel of life (resurrection).

28. Qur'án 57:3, cf. *Kitáb-i-Íqán* 161-3.

29. 'Absolute Unity' excludes all attributes because attributes are inherently the conception of the mind arrived at through a process of enumeration or division. Since the human mind cannot grasp the totality of infinitude it is necessary to build knowledge upon the enumeration of attributes or qualities. This necessary enumeration facilitates a type of limited comprehension of God which, as it happens, is the only form of comprehension of God possible to the human intellect. Such means of comprehension fall short of grasping God's true reality because all enumerations are purely abstract. For example, God's love cannot be separated from His justice, compassion, and so on. Therefore the absolute unity of God excludes all enumerations such as attributes.

30. <u>Kh</u>ájih 'Abdu'lláh: <u>Sh</u>ay<u>kh</u> Abú Ismá'íl 'Abdu'lláh Anṣárí of Hirát (1006-88 AD). One of the earliest and most eminent composers of Ṣúfí quatrains.

31. Qur'án 1:5.

32. Jalálu'd-Dín Rúmí.

33. In the *Kitáb-i-Íqán*, Bahá'u'lláh refers to the Prophets as 'the Manifestations of the Sun of Truth [God]' (pp. 14, 103, 161) and writes, some 'cleave to the obscure intricacies of knowledge, when He, Who is the Object of all knowledge, shineth as the sun' (p. 208). Here in *The Seven Valleys*, Bahá'u'lláh is conveying to the mystic seekers, and perhaps to Ṣúfís in particular, that the appearance of the divine Manifestation in this age ends the need for further reliance on whatever sources of lesser guidance to which they may have formerly turned. One uses a lamp to see at night, but once the 'Sun' (the Manifestation) has risen, there is no need for the lamp (i.e., for lesser sources of illumination) in order to see.

34. In this passage, 'Veiled from this was Moses', Jalálu'd-Dín Rúmí is referring to the biblical symbolism of Moses' request to see God's glory (Exod. 33:18), which was only partially granted. The symbolism has several meanings, but in this instance seems to indicate the complete inaccessi-

71

bility of God's essence. Since Moses was 'all strength and light' and could not see God, then how much less the ordinary seeker 'who has no wings at all'. Bahá'u'lláh writes 'all the Manifestations of His Attributes implore Him from the Sinai of Holiness to unravel His mystery' (*Gleanings* 61). In one of His own communions He writes, 'How bewildering to me, insignificant as I am, is the attempt to fathom the sacred depths of Thy knowledge' (*Gleanings* 63; cf. *World Order* 113).

35. Qur'án 2:151.

36. 'The veils of plurality' refers to the station of 'distinction' as distinguished from the station of 'essential unity' (see *Kitáb-i-Íqán* 152, 176ff). For example, in so far as religious teachings and laws progress according to the needs of particular ages, there are distinctions (i.e., differences and changes), but all these different teachings and laws reveal the same eternal truth that is exalted above all distinctions (pluralities).

37. Jalálu'd-Dín Rúmí.

38. Qur'án 4:80.

39. Qur'án 18:37.

40. The meaning of this verse, 'the variations which the wayfarer in the stages of his journey beholdeth in

the realms of being, proceed from his own vision' is expressed in other writings of Bahá'u'lláh. In the world of divinity there is essential unity and complete oneness (*tauhíd*). However, in this world differences exist in accordance with the varying capacities of the people: 'That these divine Luminaries seem to be confined at times to specific designations and attributes, as you have observed and are now observing, is due solely to the imperfect and limited comprehension of certain minds' (*Kitáb-i-Íqán* 35).

41. This reference to 'a nightingale' may refer to any Messenger of God, including Bahá'u'lláh Himself, or even to any saintly person. The subject spoken of in this paragraph is a recurring and major theme occupying much of the *Kitáb-i-Íqán* (see esp. pp. 8ff.)

42. Jalálu'd-Dín Rúmí.

43. 'gazeth only upon the place of appearance', meaning, in particular, to look only at the outward form of a religion or Manifestation of God, i.e., customs, traditions, limitations, etc., and to (consequently) fail to see the one transcendent and unlimited Source from which the religion or Manifestation originates. See e.g., *Kitáb-i-Íqán* 71-2, 124ff, 176.

44. They inflict on the Manifestations and believers 'what they themselves deserve', hence the

understanding that God's Messengers give their lives as a ransom in place of the death that we deserve, that we might have eternal life. See Rom. 5:8; Isaiah 53:5-6; 1 John 4:10; *Gleanings* 76, 315.

45. Qur'án 16:63. See *Gleanings* 76.

46. Ḥadíth, i.e., action or utterance traditionally attributed to the Prophet Muḥammad or to one of the holy Imáms.

47. 'Master of the house', cf. Matthew 24:45-50.

48. Qur'án 83:28.

49. These two points, 'The way is barred' and 'His proof is His signs; His being is His evidence' are central theological truths frequently expounded on in the Scriptures of Bahá'u'lláh. 'The way is barred' refers to the inaccessibility of God's essence, and 'His proof is His signs; His being is His evidence' means that God can only be known through His attributes. The only accessible proof of God is God's divine attributes, much as the proof of the sun is its light: 'The proof of the sun is the light thereof, which shineth and envelopeth all things' (*Kitáb-i-Íqán* 209). Every reality has some appropriate signs or characteristics by which it is identified. The same type of criterion is conveyed by Christ with the phrase 'Ye shall know them by their fruits' (Matt. 7:16ff). Cf. *Kitáb-i-Íqán* 91-2.

The point of this paragraph is taken up in almost identical words in Bahá'u'lláh's later work, the *Kitáb-i-Íqán*, see pp. 98-9.

50. A saying attributed to Muḥammad. Cf. *Gleanings* 186. The heart can reflect the attributes of divinity such as love, truthfulness, compassion and so on, and in this sense it can 'contain' God. However, God's inmost essence is forever unattainable, as Bahá'u'lláh writes, 'minds cannot grasp Me nor hearts contain Me' (*Hidden Words*, Arabic, no. 66). In the words of Solomon, 'Behold, heaven and the heaven of heavens cannot contain Thee' (1 Kings 8:27). See *Kitáb-i-Íqán* 99-104.

51. 'But for Thee, we had not known Thee', meaning that it is solely through the grace of God that He has revealed Himself in the world and opened a way through which He, the Unknown, can be known. See *Kitáb-i-Íqán* 99.

52. The 'grades of knowledge [of God] relate to the knowledge of the Manifestations of that Sun of Reality [God]'. That is, in the world of being, God can only be known through His Manifestations. See *Kitáb-i-Íqán* 99-104.

53. From the Persian poet, Ḥáfiẓ, Shamsu'd-Dín Muḥammad, of Shíráz (c. 1325 - c. 1389 AD).

54. Ḥadíth.

55. Jalálu'd-Dín Rúmí. Khiḍr (lit. green) is the name attributed to Moses' attendant (Qur'án 18:60). He has become the subject of many legends and signifies the true spiritual guide and the mysterious living wisdom of God that cannot be acquired through study.

56. Qur'án, 57:3. See also *Kitáb-i-Íqán* 159–69. Cf, Rev. 1:8, 21:6, 22:13; Heb. 13:8.

57. Jalálu'd-Dín Rúmí.

58. This 'inner land of unreality' appears to be a reference to certain metaphysical speculations of the Ṣúfís.

59. Jalálu'd-Dín Rúmí. This is a probable reference to Bahá'u'lláh's, as yet unproclaimed, station, which at that time must remain 'hidden'.

60. Qur'án 4:129.

61. Ḥáfiẓ.

62. Arabian proverb.

63. Ḥadíth.

64. Cf. Qur'án 50:21.

65. Persian mystic poem.

66. This is a title attributed to Imám 'Alí, the successor to Muḥammad (see *Kitáb-i-Íqán* 153, 167-8). The title is a claim to, or identification with, the station of Godhood (see *Kitáb-i-Íqán* 178-9). Although Imám 'Alí is not regarded in Bahá'í teachings as a supreme Manifestation of God, like Christ, Muḥammad or Bahá'u'lláh, this title could be claimed by him in two senses: first, as the successor to Muḥammad he was God's Viceregent on earth (*Epistle to the Son of the Wolf* 118, 155) and as such a reflection of God's sovereignty and second, in his life he conformed his will entirely to the will of God. Bahá'u'lláh states that absolute conformity to the will of God is the meaning of the claim to Godhood. 'This station is the station in which one dieth to himself and liveth in God. Divinity, whenever I mention it, indicateth My complete and absolute self-effacement' (*Epistle to the Son of the Wolf* 41). See also *Kitáb-i-Íqán* 180.

67. Imám 'Alí.

68. Luqmán is a philosopher or sage who appears to have been known among the Arabs during the time of Muḥammad (see the Qur'án, Surah of Luqmán: 'we bestowed wisdom upon Luqmán', Qur'án 31:11). See also the *Mathnaví* of Jalálu'd-Dín Rúmí, Book II.

69. Luqmán explains to his son, in the form of a verbal puzzle, that just as he cannot avoid sleeping, so he cannot avoid dying, but just as he awakens each

day from sleep, so will he enjoy life after dying.

70. Jalálu'd-Dín Rúmí.

71. Literally 'Jayhún', a river in Turkistán.

72. Qur'án 9:51.

73. 'Ancient of Days' refers to God, or He who represents God in the world of creation. Cf. Dan. 7:9, 13, 22; *Kitáb-i-Íqán* 99.

74. Jalálu'd-Dín Rúmí.

75. Qur'án 76:5.

76. Words attributed to Muḥammad. This theme is expounded by Bahá'u'lláh in the *Kitáb-i-Íqán* (130-2).

77. Qur'án 55:26, 27.

78. Qur'án 15:21.

79. 'city', i.e., City of God. See *Kitáb-i-Íqán* 199.

80. Farídu'd-Dín 'Aṭṭár.

81. Ḥadíth.

82. Jalálu'd-Dín Rúmí.

83. Pantheism, a Ṣúfí doctrine derived from the formula: 'Only God exists; He is in all things, and all things are in Him.'

84. This refers to the tendency among some Ṣúfís to delineate three hierarchical stages in the spiritual life of a seeker: 1. religious Laws (*Sharí'at*); 2. the spiritual Path (*Taríqat*) on which the mystic seeker journeys in search of the True One, a stage which sometimes includes withdrawal and seclusion from society; 3. the innermost Truth (*Haqíqat*) which, to the Ṣúfí, is always the goal of the journey. In this passage, Bahá'u'lláh counters the belief that the seeker can reach a stage in which he or she no longer needs to follow the religious law. The law is essential to fostering and preserving wellbeing and harmony in the community, and hence it cannot be dispensed with.

85. Qur'án 17:81: 'Observe prayer at sunset, till the first darkening of the night, and the daybreak reading - for the daybreak reading hath its witnesses, and watch unto it in the night: this shall be an excess in service: it may be that thy Lord will raise thee to a glorious station . . .'

86. Qur'án 2:84.

87. Persian mystic poem.

88. Salám, meaning '*Peace*', as in the Hebrew '*Shalom*'.

89. Arabian proverb.

90. The five letters of the Persian alphabet composing the word 'Gunjishk' are *G, N, J, Sh* and *K*, i.e., *Gáf, Nún, Jím, Shín* and *Káf.* The method of interpretation Bahá'u'lláh is using is somewhat unusual but is in some ways parallel to other existing approaches such as the ancient practice of geometria, whereby the hidden esoteric meaning of Scripture is thought to be accessible through the numerical value of words. Although Bahá'u'lláh sometimes makes use of such equations, such methods are not given prominence in His teachings and He rejects the idea that esoteric interpretations should ever take precedence over the literal meaning of revealed Law.

In this instance, concerning Shaykh Muḥyi'd-Dín's comments on the meaning of the type of bird 'Gunjishk' - possibly a reference to the sparrow mentioned in 'Aṭṭár's *Conference of the Birds* - Bahá'u'lláh is using a similar, but much freer interpretative approach. As the text indicates, Muḥyí'd-Dín has shown in his interpretation that he is well grounded in mystic learning. Bahá'u'lláh's interpretative approach appears to be deliberately simplistic to demonstrate that, without reliance on a complicated hermeneutical formula, a door leading to God can be seen in what appears to be an ordinary sparrow. Each letter is simply connected to a principal term relevant to the life of faith. The interpretative method is as significant as the interpretation itself. Both stress the opening goal of *The Seven Valleys*, which is: God hath given teachings 'to the end' that 'none shall contemplate anything whatsoever but that he shall see God therein'.

91. This and the foregoing quotations are from the teachings of Islám.

92. This appears to be a reference to Bahá'u'lláh. Cf. *Kitáb-i-Íqán* 78, 175, 257.

SELECTED
BIBLIOGRAPHY

Bahá'u'lláh. *The Book of Certitude (Kitáb-i-Íqán).* Trans.
Shoghi Effendi. Wilmette, Ill.: Bahá'í Publishing
Trust, 1931, 3rd edn., 1974.

—— *Epistle to the Son of the Wolf.* Trans. Shoghi Effendi.
Wilmette, Ill.: Bahá'í Publishing Trust, 1941, 3rd
edn., 1976.

—— *Gleanings from the Writings of Bahá'u'lláh.* Trans.
Shoghi Effendi. Wilmette, Ill.: Bahá'í Publishing
Trust, 1939, 2nd edn., 1956.

—— *The Hidden Words.* Trans. Shoghi Effendi. London:
Oneworld Publications, 1986.

—— *Tablets of Bahá'u'lláh revealed after the Kitáb-i-Aqdas.*
Comp. Research Department of the Universal House
of Justice, trans. Habib Taherzadeh and a Committee
at the Bahá'í World Centre. Haifa, Israel: Bahá'í
World Centre, 1978.

Shoghi Effendi. *God Passes By.* Wilmette, Ill.: Bahá'í
Publishing Trust, 1944, 1974.

—— *The World Order of Bahá'u'lláh.* Wilmette, Ill.: Bahá'í
Publishing Trust, 1938, 2nd edn., 1974.